SOPHIA LOREN

SOPHIA LOREN

IN THE CAMERA EYE

PHOTOGRAPHY AND COMMENTARY BY **SAM SHAW**

Hamlyn

London • New York • Sydney • Toronto

Published by
THE HAMLYN PUBLISHING GROUP LIMITED 1980
London • New York • Sydney • Toronto
Astronaut House, Feltham, Middlesex, England

ISBN 0 600 34155 0

Printed in the United States of America

Entire project supervised by Sam Shaw

Cover Design, title page by Jacques Chazaud

Graphic Production by Filmar Graphics, Inc., San Diego, California

Photo Credits
Sam Shaw
Cover, title page, 7, 9-125, 127, 153, back cover
UPI
128-159
Hy Simon Sunday Features Syndication
151 (top), 160

CONTENTS

1   FOREWORD   8

2   SOPHIA LOREN: IN THE CAMERA EYE   12

3   SOPHIA LOREN: HER LIFE   128
     The Girl Who Won The Prize
     The Hungry Years
     Quo Vadis
     Ponti . . . Always Ponti
     The Pride and the Passion
     Shaping Up
     Sophia's Sister
     The Villa Ponti
     Two Women
     One of Us
     From Sex Symbol to Artist
     Mama Sophia
     After 20 Years

4   THE FILMS OF SOPHIA LOREN   154

FOREWORD

The following candid photographs and recollections are my homage to Sophia Loren.

My photographs of her date to the early 1950's, when movie tycoon Carlo Ponti, soon to become her husband, took control of her career. The earliest shots of Sophia show her in the apartment bought for her by Carlo; her first sumptuous home (which, characteristically, she opened to her mother, to her younger sister, to her poor cousins).

Afterward, I photographed Sophia often; and over the years, in the course of working together, she and I became friends.

As in the lives of all human beings, the lives of film stars have bright moments and dark ones. My tribute to Sophia reflects happy moments in her life.

The camera falls in love with certain faces. The camera lens (its "eye"), finds the secret, the special magnetism or charisma, in these faces. The camera loves Sophia.

For me, Loren summons up certain lucid, lasting images. In my eyes:

She is off the walls of the House of Mysteries at Pompeii.

She is the goddess of fertility in the Naples museum.

She is the pizza girl in De Sica's "The Gold of Naples."

She is a masked Venetian beauty, painted by Longhi.

She is an Italian peasant, carrying a loaded basket upon her head.

She is earth, poetry, art, life.

She is a movie star . . . and every woman!

SAM SHAW

SOPHIA LOREN: IN THE CAMERA EYE

2

11

Loren's childhood in wartime Italy was turbulent. She had a difficult time.

She talks about it. She tells us about it. She's written about it.

Not only her, many young Italian women. A lot of them gave themselves for K-rations, silk stockings, cigarettes, chewing gum. These are the ugly facts of war.

Loren's an Italian woman: she has all their qualities.

A tremendous maternal instinct . . . She can be 14, a mother . . . a mother goddess.

Tremendous, undying loves.

Tremendous family ties.

She takes on the burden of her kind: during times of

stress she will take care of a little brother or little sister as
well and as efficiently as her mother; she will take care
of her cousins as well.

Loren probably has it in her book (I haven't read it), but
her great love is her mother. She will protect her mother
from the world, from society, from any ill wind that blows.

Not only her mother, her sister.

Not only her sister, her cousins . . .

Before she made "The Pride and the Passion" we made a
little short. I shot her at home — her first luxurious
apartment. There's a photograph of her in that house
with all her cousins living there with her.

Her mother was mother to her then; and she was
mother to her mother. She still is mother to her mother.

An Italian woman . . . all their qualities. . .

KODAK SAFETY FILM ++

Sophia's mother (R) and sister Maria (L).

Sophia's first luxurious apartment...

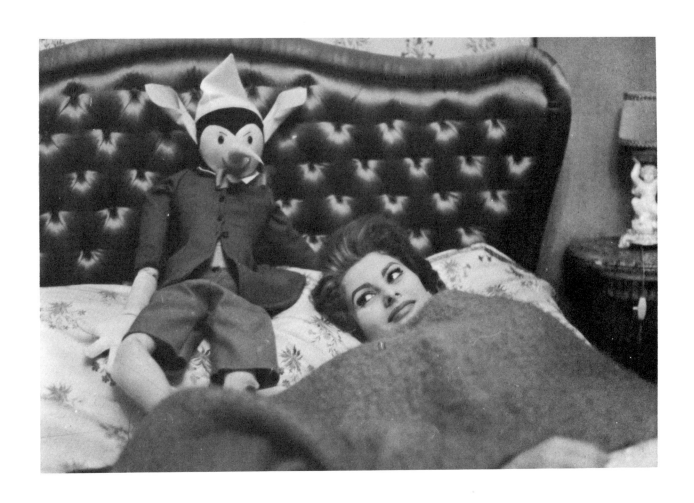

Sophia's sister Maria (l.), and her cousin Patrezia

Sophia told me once, "Posing for the camera is a love affair." And that's true; she falls in love at that moment. The camera loves her and she loves the camera. And the camera can't make a mistake, and she can't make a mistake.

But she's a woman like that in life, too . . . So sure of her beauty that she doesn't ask the right of censorship on pictures, never asks.

For instance: I did a photo-essay; famous personalities and their recipies. She did a thing for me on cooking eggplant. In one shot, a little oil hit her; she blinked and she screwed up her face, looked like a clown. Yet she wouldn't think of censoring that picture. She thought it humorous and had a big laugh.

She's got another self that looks upon herself. She can look at herself from a distance.

"Posing for the camera is a love affair."

Basilio Franchina (c.), whom Sophia calls her closest friend, who's given
important help in her professional life.

She's a woman like that in life, too...

in the background,

me with camera!

Shubert (c.),
the most popular fashion designer in Rome
at the start of Sophia's career.

. . .another self that looks upon herself. . .

Sophia's magnificently beautiful. Handsome. Amazonian.

And she continues to grow in beauty with maturity.

She has a lot of self-confidence; she's a beauty who knows she's a beauty.

Sophia accepting her beauty is like Joe DiMaggio accepting his prowess as a ballplayer. Easy grace — you don't have to force it. Joe has that inner confidence; he doesn't have to prove himself . . . Sugar Ray Robinson has it . . . The real great ones don't have to say they're great. Their records stand for them.

I've seen Sophia in a rented house in Beverly Hills, with everything a woman could want. Beauty. Talent. Wealth. Love. Everything except her country; but she herself always was — and is — her country.

in "The Pride and the Passion"

Growing in beauty with maturity. . .

...a beauty who knows she's a beauty...

. . . in Beverly Hills . . .

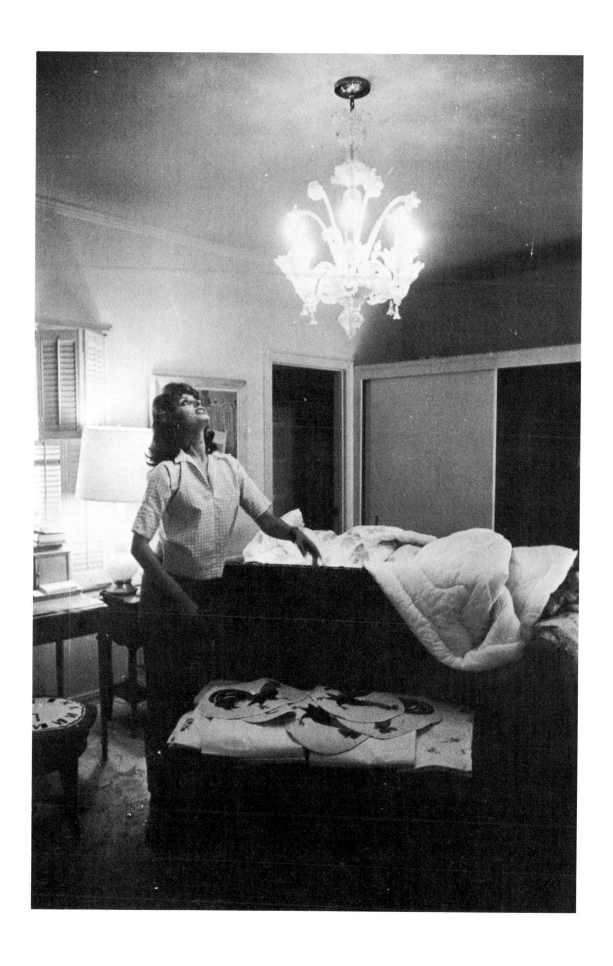

Everything except her country; but she herself always was
— and is — her country...

Leaving normal school at an early age, she knew Leopardi, D'Annunzio, Manzoni, Cavour, Verdi . . .

Italians are surrounded as kids by Michaelangelo, by DaVinci, by Roman ruins. Just as Greeks are surrounded by the ruins of antiquity, the statues, the Parthenon. That's what they're brought up on; you don't have to train them to appreciate it, it's part of their lives . . .

I remember being brought up in "Little Italy," Mott Street. Subway workers, pavement guys, sanitation men, grocery men, butchers; they knew every opera. They would stand at the opera in the Met. They were the balcony in the Met. All you heard in the buildings were Caruso and Gigli records. You were brought up with that culture, whether you were in the streets or not . . .

But it wasn't just opera. Many jazz players in the American jazz renaissance were second generation Italians . . .

Sophia loves American jazz, loves jazz. It's too
bad Duke died. She was going to make a record with
Duke Ellington. He was itching to write something with
her.

She loves to sing. She could sing blues and jazz. (She did
a movie once, "Aida." But they didn't use her voice. It
was Renata Tibaldi's.)

I think that's Sophia's ambition — to make a blues or
jazz record.

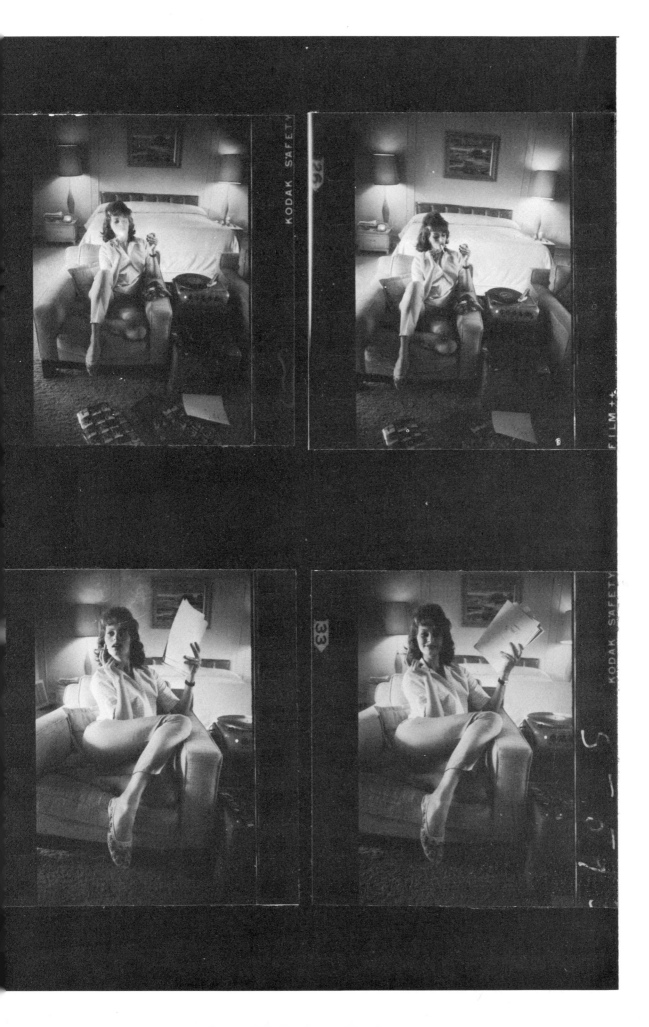

67

She has a terrific relationship with Carlo.

I think the origin of the relationship was in the competition between Carlo Ponti and Dino DeLaurentiis to create a star. It's a business; you've got to create a star. How do you create a star and control them? You marry them. DeLaurentiis took Silvana Mangano, and Carlo went out to create somebody bigger, better than Silvana Mangano, and got Sophia . . .

Ponti is a well educated man, a very cultured person, charming. Combination of cultured person, business person; an international type, an international type in pictures . . .

Pulp literature, the popular woman's magazines, advertising, Hollywood movies so impress, so brainwash the public, the audience, that it's inevitable that Clark Gable should be with Vivien Leigh. Or a Tyrone Power and another beautiful dame should be the perfect combination.

Sophia's such a beautiful woman that on paper the ideal magazine cover would be her and Cary Grant. Or the ideal way to sell soap or perfume would be to have a couple like that. These are romantic notions of what romance is. Fairy tales . . .

Artists, writers and directors weave through the life Loren and Ponti lead; Alberto Moravia, Mario Soldati, Federico Fellini. De Sica, an intimate working relationship. Basilio Franchina — my God! With Moravia, he wrote the first story expressly made for Sophia, "Woman of the River."

Carlo Ponti.

Cary Grant.

Vittorio de Sica.

Loren is an artist. Dead serious, instinctive . . . Learning all the time, giving everything to every role.

Actresses who take their roles seriously are all the same. They all go through the same thing; transposition of character, development of character.

Tony Quinn says, "You put on another skin. When you're through with a role, you shed that skin and take on another one."

Underneath that shedding of the skin, putting off the skin, every actor or actress goes through the same emotionally traumatic experience . . .

Actresses have some universal characteristics that their
work imposes on them, that their living imposes on
them. Acting's a trade, an inherited trade. The very
nature of the work brings out traits.

They all have suicide within them . . .

Sophia is a rare exception.

Carlo's protected her all the way.

80

learning all the time . . .

giving everything to every

role. . .

Every actress goes through the same emotionally
traumatic experience. . .

Pure motion pictures don't need actors. Luigi Zampa, the great Italian director, told me that.

We were in Naples. Somebody stopped him in the street, started talking, wanted a part.

When he left, Zampa said:

"This guy — I can't use him in a picture. He's in Italian music hall; the professional Italian actor is terrible in motion pictures. But the Italian citizen, the guy off the street, so lacking in personal inhibitions, so very extroverted, he's a terrific motion picture actor. He doesn't have to look at the camera. He's himself; not self-conscious, not bottled up."

Same thing with Sophia . . .

In the accidental selection of somebody you put in front of the camera you discover happily that they can sustain the magic — no matter what occurs.

Sophia's got a fantastic magic, which few others have.

Sophia's got a fantastic magic. . .

Beyond instinct, Sophia learned a lot from De Sica; and Blasetti, another great Italian director.

De Sica taught her the craft of acting. Secrets of interpretation, restraint. He was a director who knew the craft of acting better than anyone else.

Did you ever see him act? Ever see De Sica on the screen? One of the greatest actors of all time.

It took a director like him to get the talent out of her.

He could get it out of a small kid. He took it out of a man who was a factory worker; "Bicycle Thief," the father — what a performance!

How he got a role and made something out of it!

Then "Umberto D!" The little man who was a professor. What he did with "Umberto D!" Really the portrayal of his own father.

That picture: I took John Cassavettes to see that in the screenings. We both wept like hell! Wept!

De Sica taught her the craft of acting.

De Sica coaching Marcello Mastroianni, Sophia's co-star in many pictures

It took De Sica to get the talent out of her...

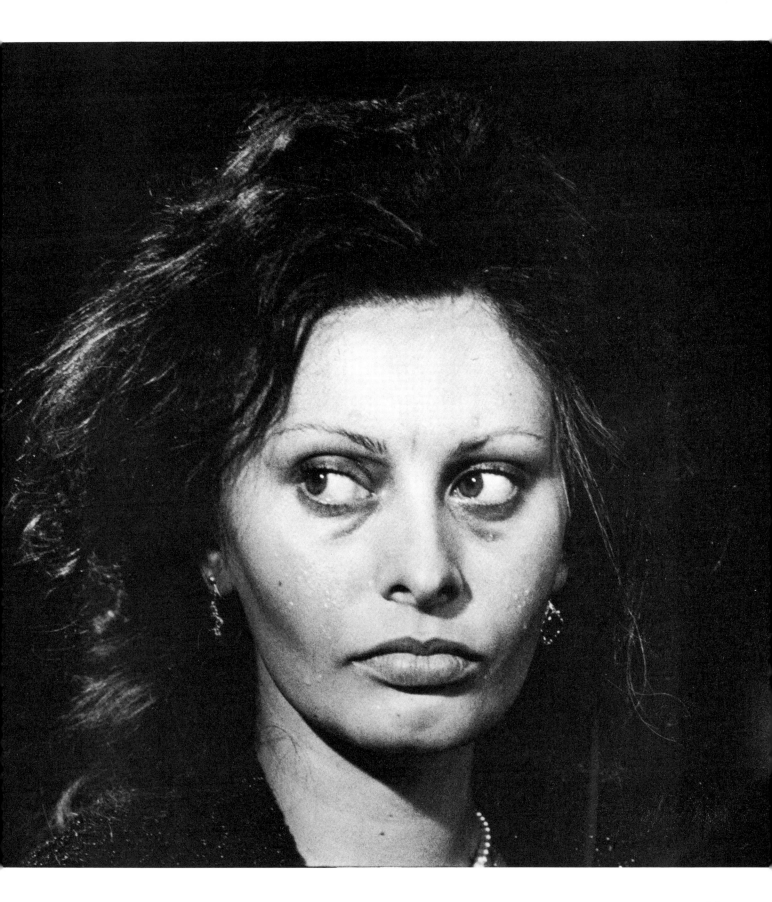

In the beginning, when Sophia knew that as an actress she was going to crack the Hollywood scene, she studied languages. English, French.

She picked up English so quickly you couldn't believe it! With an English coach, reading the poems of T.S. Eliot.

She has a great ear, a great ear . . .

Loren never had a good role until she did "Two Women." Before that she did a lot of commercial pictures. They broke all over the world, but they were never artistic pictures.

Even today she makes pot-boilers, one right after
another, and makes a million dollars for each picture.
And she's worth it!

These pictures might be disasters in America, but they
break box office records everywhere else in the world.
"Two Women" was an artistic hit, but it didn't make the
millions that other pictures made.

As Quinn did in "La Strada," Sophia in "Two Women"
showed the world she could act — in the grand tradition
of Magnani . . .

with Stanley Kramer, her first American director

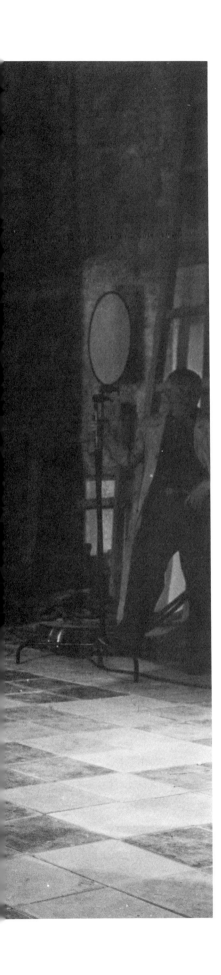

As the years go by, Loren grows as an actress and as a woman. She's grown intellectually on a scale equal to that of her beauty. She's developing a tremendous range.

Whatever she does on screen is right. She can do ordinary pictures; and still she remains an international superstar, still she grows as a human being. Actors and actresses don't walk through a role; they do the best that they can.

She doesn't worry. She's sure of herself. She doesn't care whether her back is to the camera. She doesn't fight to steal a scene.

As the years go by, Loren grows as an actress and as a woman...

in De Sica's "Marriage Italian Style"

Whatever she does

on screen is right.

In shooting a picture, you sometimes shoot the end in the beginning; sometimes you shoot the beginning at the end. Pictures are often shot out of sequence.

The actors and actresses must remember lines immediately, and feel the development of characters.

Loren's very disciplined. She has intense concentration; wipes everything out.

It's very distracting: lights, electricians, people moving, people gawking . . .

It could be the hottest emotional scene — and a member of the crew will be up in the flies reading a newspaper. He's done his job, done the light, taken care of it.

Nearly every picture I've worked on, I've shot something like that.

You think that couldn't be distracting to an actress who's an artist? You've got to shut all those things out.

She has intense concentration;

wipes everything out...

It's very distracting: lights, electricians, people moving, people gawking. . .

It could be the hottest emotional scene...

SOPHIA LOREN: HER LIFE

3

The Girl Who Won The Prize

In 1932, a contest was held in Italy — to discover an exact double for Greta Garbo. The winner of that contest was Romilda Villani. She won a ticket to Hollywood and a screen test.

For many other girls, this would have been the fulfillment of a dream. But for Romilda, it turned into a nightmare. Her parents refused to let her go to Hollywood. Her ambitions to become an actress were shattered.

A few years later, she had a child — a daughter. The girl was born out of wedlock. Friends and relatives insisted that the child should be given to an orphanage. But Romilda refused. Through years of poverty, disgrace, war, she helped her child to grow and mature.

The mother and child grew strong together, fighting at first for survival. Then for the fame that Romilda was unable to achieve.

Today, Romilda Villani lives in luxury and basks — deservedly — in the fame and success of her daughter . . . Sophia Loren.

The Hungry Years

Sophia Loren was born in a charity hospital in Rome in 1934. While she was an infant, her mother barely made a living giving piano lessons. They survived by the grace of their relatives. Sunday at Grandma's house was the one wholesome meal of the week.

When she went to school, the other girls called Sophia "toothpick." This, and the fact that she did not have a father (everyone knew that her mother had borne her out of wedlock) made school very difficult. She would arrive at the last minute — just before classes began — to avoid the other girls' taunts.

Sophia did not meet her father, Riccardo Scicolone, until she was five. At that time, Romilda Villani phoned him in Rome to tell him that his little girl was terribly sick. Scicolone rushed to where Sophia and her mother lived, only to find out that Sophia was not sick. He was furious.

Though he refused to marry Romilda, he remained in touch with her and the little girl. Three years after Sophia was born, her sister Maria was also born. Again, Scicolone was the father; again, the child was born out of wedlock.

Throughout Sophia's youth, she knew that her mother truly loved Riccardo; she also knew that Riccardo would never become her legal father. Nevertheless, her father gave her his name. (She was also to adopt the name of Lazarro, before finding her screen name, Loren.)

Sophia Loren makes her first Communion.

128

During those days of war, Sophia learned of the atrocities of the Germans. She saw German soldiers, first as friends, and then as enemies. She recalls seeing the Germans shooting civilians — almost as sport.

She saw the horrors of war firsthand; the hunger, the brutality. Through it all, she developed a sense of survival that remains with her to this day.

Sophia checks out the vegetables; a man checks her out, 1954.

The family lived together in Pozzuoli, a small town outside of Naples. They were poor, very religious. But looking through the torn curtains of her living room, little Sophia would see the sea — blue and beautiful.

In 1940, war came to Pozzuoli. At first, it brought prosperity, then disaster.

A munitions plant stood in the center of town. Night after night, Allied bombs exploded over the entire area — while the townspeople took refuge in a dark tunnel.

Sophia remembers those days with mixed emotions. There was terror, of course, and a sense that death and destruction were everywhere. There was also a sense of unity: huddled together in the dark tunnel, while the bombs blasted overhead, everyone sang and told jokes and laughed to dispel the fear and gloom.

For the first time, little Sophia felt she belonged.

Finally, the bombings became too severe. The whole town was ordered evacuated — north. Sophia and her family went to live near Naples with cousins who hardly knew them.

After her success in "Aida" (1953), Sophia visits GI's in Italy to learn American ways prior to a visit to Hollywood.

Typical cheesecake pose released before "Two Women"

Romilda knew that her daughter needed preparation for the career she desired for her. She taught her to play the piano, taught her to walk, taught her all the rules of polite society.

Quo Vadis

In 1948, when Sophia was barely 16, a beauty contest was held near the town of Pozzuoli. First prize was two tickets to Rome. Sophia's mother decided it was time to test her judgement — she entered her daughter in the contest. Sophia won.

But her mother decided to hold the tickets until Sophia was older and had acquired some skill as an actress. She sent Sophia to acting school. Then something unexpected happened.

He mother heard that a huge Hollywood film, "Quo Vadis," was being shot in Rome —

Sophia as local fish seller who nets her man in "Scandal in Sorrento" (1955).

When the Allies conquered Italy, the family was allowed to return to Pozzuoli. Her mother's resourcefulness again came into play. She opened her home to the American soldiers, played the piano for them to make them feel that there — thousands of miles from their real homes — was another home they might enjoy.

The year was 1945. Sophia was eleven. She observed, appreciatively, as her mother did everything that was necessary to keep the family together.

After the war, there were still long periods of cold and hunger; periods when merely surviving took all the power and resourcefulness you could muster.

During this time, Sophia — shy and withdrawn — would spend hours watching films from Hollywood. Here was a totally strange and wonderful world. A world where Fred Astaire and Ginger Rogers danced, where Charlie Chaplin got slapped in the face with a pie and everyone laughed, where fantasy became a wonderful reality.

Meanwhile, Sophia's schoolmates had

thousands of extras were being hired. She and Sophia immediately packed up and took the train to Rome.

The casting call was total chaos. Even though a "cast of thousands," literally was needed, there were far more people who wanted a job than any studio could hire. The screaming and pushing were intense. When the dust settled, Sophia and her mother had both been hired as extras.

After the filming, Sophia decided to stay on as a model, while her mother returned home. She lived in a small room and made a few friends.

In order to survive, she would take any job that came her way: film extra . . . model . . . clerk.

Sophia was in Rome, determined that she would not leave until she had gained the success she desired. She had inherited her mother's dreams . . . her mother's drive . . . and her mother's beauty.

Charles Boyer is handy when Sophia needs a light in "Lucky to be a Woman" (1955).

Charles Boyer, playing a press agent in "Lucky to be a Woman" (1955), sets Sophia for a publicity shot.

Ponti . . . Always Ponti

Sophia had been in Rome for just a few months. She modeled for the cartoon-like "fumetti" — an Italian version of the soap opera, which appeared regularly in Rome's newspapers. But she barely made a living at it.

One evening, Sophia and several friends decided to splurge. "Let's go to the Colle Oppio," one suggested. "They're holding a beauty contest for Miss Rome . . ."

Sophia agreed. It was the turning point of her life.

She sat at the table, enjoying her plate of pasta. One of the judges came over and asked if she would consider entering the beauty contest. She said no. The man left and sat down.

A few minutes later he returned — and urged her once again to enter the contest. Apparently, one of the other judges thought that she could win. "Which one of the judges?" Sophia asked. The man pointed. Sophia turned her head, and for the first time in her life she smiled at the famous film producer Carlo Ponti.

Ponti returned the smile. Sophia entered the beauty contest — and won second place. She also won a screen test with Ponti.

The screen test took place the following day. It was an utter disaster. Sophia couldn't act, couldn't walk, couldn't do anything right. Carlo had faith in her, however, and insisted that she return in a few weeks for another test . . . with a new cameraman.

The next time, the results were equally bad. Ponti continued to have faith in her. He insisted that she return and take yet another test. It, too, was a disaster.

Nevertheless, Ponti decided to give his young protege bit parts in some pot-boilers. Sophia worked as an extra in "The White Slave Trade" . . . "The Dream of Zorro" . . . "Hearts Upon the Sea" . . . "Bluebeard's Six Wives" and "It's Him, Yes! Yes!" She was a teenager; yet with Ponti's guidance she was learning the film business.

At the age of 18, Sophia landed the first important role of her life: "Aida". Gina Lollobrigida had signed to play the title role in this film version of Verdi's opera. Then she discovered

Wearing native dress, Sophia dances the flamenco after hours during filming of "The Pride and the Passion" (1957).

that she would be doing lip-sync while Renata Tebaldi did the actual singing. Lollobrigida wanted out. The film was ready to roll. Ponti called Sophia to play the part.

She was magnificent! Without uttering a word of her own, she made an unforgettable

In matador's costume for "The Pride and the Passion" (1957).

Exhausted after first encounter with the bull ring.

Between takes Sophia picks up pointers on bullfighting.

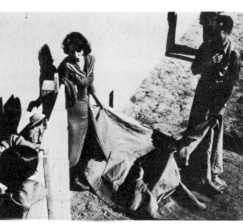

Drying off in "Boy on a Dolphin" (1957).

Sophia and director Jean Negulesco chat on the set of "Boy on a Dolphin" (1957).

impact. The film version of "Aida" was distributed throughout the world — and Sophia, overnight, became a sensation. Ponti immediately signed Sophia to a personal contract.

In subsequent films, Sophia (who had now changed her name from Lazarro to Loren) clearly demonstrated that she had the figure and know-how to dominate the screen as a sex goddess. There was hardly a hint, though, that she would evolve into a serious actress until 1953. It was then that she made "The Anatomy of Love" — and the first time she co-starred with Marcello Mastroianni. The cinematic electricity between the two was immediate and explosive.

The team of Loren and Mastroianni returned in "Too Bad She's Bad" — one of her earliest hits. "The Miller's Wife" followed, an artistic as well as box-office triumph.

Carlo decided it was time for his protege to break the image which Italian films had created for Sophia. He wanted her to make her first English language film, and patiently searched for two years before he found a suitable vehicle for Sophia. Finally, in 1957, Ponti found the "right" film, the vehicle destined to catapult Sophia Loren to superstardom; "The Pride and the Passion".

Again, Carlo had made the right decision for Sophia. Throughout their association, she had trusted him totally. And her trust had been amply justified. Each time that her career reached a pivotal point, it was Ponti who decided where she would go and what she would do next. Each time, his judgement was correct.

After "The Pride and the Passion", Ponti felt that Sophia was ready for a truly serious drama. She made "Desire Under the Elms" with Tony Perkins, settling once and for all the question of whether or not Sophia Loren was an actress of the first magnitude.

The Pride and the Passion

In 1957, Stanley Kramer was casting for "The Pride and the Passion". Two male leads were chosen: Cary Grant and Frank Sinatra. Only the female lead remained to be filled.

There were rumors that Ava Gardner would

Waiting for the next take in "Legend of the Lost" (1957).

The marriage was not recognized; instead, Carlo and Sophia were accused of bigamy, a charge that eventually forced the couple to change their legal residence to France.

Legal or not, the marriage between Sophia and Carlo has been one of the strongest in the film world.

One of the things the public finds hard to understand is what Sophia sees in Carlo Ponti, who is twenty years older and several inches shorter than she.

Shortly after their marriage, people raised the question. She replied. "What nobody could understand then and still can't is the extraordinary power of the man. He generates a tremendous excitement for me. He is a sensitive lover, a cultured friend, the understanding father I never had. Every woman's needs are wrapped up inside that man . . . all my needs anyway!"

Gold of Naples

"I think the most important part of my career is when I met my husband," said Sophia, "and then the second man of my life is Vittorio De Sica."

Indeed, it was Ponti who first coached Sophia, transforming her slowly, carefully into star material. He knew that she could do so much

get the role, but Carlo Ponti wanted this to be Sophia's first English-language movie. After a few conversations with Kramer, the announcement was made: Sophia Loren would get the role.

A huge party was held by Kramer, before the filming began. It was the very first time that Sophia met Grant.

Throughout the filming of "The Pride and the Passion", Grant and Loren were often seen together. Grant admitted that he was head over heels in love with Sophia.

Sophia remembered the words that her mother had spoken to her about Carlo Ponti: "He's a married man . . . you will waste your time waiting for him . . . he has a wife and children . . . find someone else."

Pictures of Grant and Loren appeared increasingly in tabloids from Hollywood to Rome, stirring speculation. The pictures were just what Carlo Ponti needed to act. He made up his mind; he would divorce his wife and marry Sophia.

But how? The answer: divorce by proxy and marriage by proxy.

In Catholic Italy, official reaction was swift.

Dealing with rough lovers John Wayne and Rossano Brazzi in "Legend of the Lost" (1957).

Carlo visits Sophia on location in Lybia during the filming of "Legend of the Lost" (1957).

more than pose. Had she been left to others, she may never have realized her potential; she sought to do everything she could to further her talent, but it was Ponti who knew what she had to do, and Ponti who guided her in doing it.

When Ponti had brought Sophia to a certain point, when she was more polished as an actress than she had been when they met, he introduced her to Vittorio De Sica — a man who had distinguished himself through his ability to shape raw talent.

Sophia was then like an uncut gem. De Sica signed her for "Gold of Naples" without even giving her a screen test. Asked to explain what he saw in her that prompted him to take such an unorthodox step, he declared, "A revelation. She was created differently, behaved differently, affected me differently from any woman I have known. I looked at that face, those unbelievable eyes, and I saw it all as a miracle."

As a postscript, De Sica was quick to point out that his feelings about Sophia had always been purely paternal.

"I am not really a director," he said, "just a teacher of elocution. I know how to make people say their lines. And Sophia is clever. She understands this so well with her intuition."

Together she and De Sica became an incomparable team. One writer commented, "it was a performance in itself" when De Sica directed Sophia. She said, "De Sica taught me you can't paint your way into a scene."

Sophia went to Hollywood against De Sica's will. She wanted the glamour, the American fan adoration; De Sica felt this was the worst segment of her career, with the exception of "Desire Under the Elms", which she made with Burl Ives and Anthony Perkins. He summed up her Hollywood foray simply: "She made bad pictures; it was a bad period for her." There are those who would disagree, but for De Sica, Sophia was a Neapolitan, the essential Italian woman. Hollywood, for De Sica, was not fit for comparison with Italy.

When De Sica was ready to film "Two Women", he wired Sophia, who was then in England. The film had originally been planned to star Anna Magnani as the mother and Sophia as the daughter. Although she was only 27-years-old, Sophia had to play the part of a woman nearly 40-years-old who looked and felt older. De Sica asked her to play the part with "no make-up, nothing at all." "Have the courage to become this character," he urged her. "I guarantee that you will give a wonderful interpretation of it."

Sophia's rendition of this role won her the Silver Ribbon (the Italian "Oscar"), The Best Actress Award at Cannes, The New York Film Critics' Award as Best Foreign Actress, and of course, the coveted Oscar from the American Motion Picture Academy.

It was reported that Sophia felt the role so deeply that she broke down in tears several times. She modestly claims that it was one of the easiest roles she has played. "The character was so strong," she said, "nothing could destroy it. Also, I was working within the range of my own experience."

De Sica said, "Though I taught her, directed every move, when the tears came and the anguish in the film, it was her heart, her soul, her own experience that she was drawing on. And when I saw it, I realized that she had come back to Italy. She had come back to me with this vital desire to re-express herself in her own language."

Shaping Up

As a child, Sophia was always considered serious, dedicated, intense. When she launched her career as an actress, these qualities helped her rise above the norm.

Make an appointment with Sophia, and she will always be on time. (She once scolded a reporter for LIFE magazine for being a half-hour late: "You have very bad manners.")

Working on a film, she spends her spare time learning, studying, rehearsing. During takes, she rarely flubs her lines.

Before making her first English-language film, "The Pride and the Passion", she learned English with the aid of the producer's wife by reading the poems of T.S. Eliot.

"When Sophia decided to learn English, she started at the top," quipped one of her co-stars.

A thorough professional, Sophia Loren expects all her co-stars to be professional as well — even if they are only children.

When child actor Paul Peterson kept giggling during a scene (in the movie, "Houseboat") in which he was supposed to cry, Sophia took command of the situation. She went up to Paul, took him aside, shook him gently, and said,

Loren and Carlo return to Los Angeles to continue filming "Houseboat" (1958) after proxy marriage in Mexico.

Knitting to pass time between scenes in "Desire Under the Elms" (1958).

"Listen, Paul! They're giving you a lot of money to do this and if you don't pay attention then they shouldn't pay you. I'm working hard, why don't you?"

Needless to say, this unexpected treatment worked; Paul had no trouble crying during the next take.

Directors, producers, and co-stars soon realized that Sophia could often be so involved with her work that she took no time to "play."

After filming "The Pride and the Passion" for Stanley Kramer, Sophia flew to Rome — bypassing Kramer's lavish end-of-movie cast party. The filming done, she simply considered her job finished.

In each role, Sophia has become more

fascinated with the business of acting — and more devoted to the art of film.

She has described her favorite roles on screen as "passionate, tragic parts, strong, highly emotional people." But off-screen, it's a different matter. She once told the Italian writer Alberto Moravia: "In life, I'd like to be just the opposite of what I am in art, cool and collected, with a strong inner life."

Those who know her well believe she has achieved both ambitions.

Sophia's Sister

Maria, Sophia's younger sister, was born in 1938. When they were growing up, Sophia's mother tried to treat them equally. Since they lived in a world where actual survival was in question, minor problems and small disagreements between them didn't matter.

An equality is created when children are hungry; when everyone is shivering with cold; when you huddle together as bombs destroy homes and possibly people you know. An equality born out of hardship and war. A shared experience —something Sophia and her sister still remember.

Ironically, that shared memory is today tinged with nostalgia. Sophia recalls a great feeling of unity when she and Maria huddled together in the tunnel in Pozzuoli.

Of course, their lives were in danger. But it was a danger everyone shared. Of course, there was fear and mutual anger. But these were feelings everyone had.

The sense of togetherness that she learned as a child has stood Sophia in good stead as an adult. The humanity she learned in days of war is amply evident in her acting. There is an earthiness about the woman that bespeaks a triumph over hardship.

When Sophia grew rich and famous, she also shared her wealth and fame with all the members of her family.

When Maria's marriage stirred controversy (her wedding to Romano Mussolini, son of the former Italian Fascist dictator, was front page

Smiling broadly, Sophia and Carlo leave Christian Dior's after buying dresses and shoes. The couple was heading for London, for the premiere of "The Key" (1958).

Sophia at surprise birthday party given for her by three youngsters working with her on "Houseboat" (1958).

Embracing Anthony Quinn in "The Black Orchid" (1959).

choirs of ancient Italian cathedrals), a 17-foot fireplace designed by the modern British sculptor Henry Moore, a small cinema room, an antique bed reputed to have once been British Prime Minister Anthony Eden's, and a table made of marble from the villa's catacombs.

To this add antique furnishings of all kinds and an abundance of artwork.

In the midst of so much luxury, Sophia still enjoys simple things most: to lie on the floor and roll around with her two children . . . to tickle them until they laugh with glee . . . to walk barefoot.

And she still recalls that the most delicious food she ever tasted was the glass of goat's milk she enjoyed as a child, when she was hungry.

Thus, in spite of her vast wealth and world-wide fame, Sophia Loren remains the simple, sensitive and direct woman she always was.

Carlo Ponti once said of their lavish villa: "I like to know it exists, that there's a place I can stay."

But Sophia is less comfortable with their grand surroundings. "Even now, with all this, I never feel totally secure. Everything one has, one can lose."

news), Sophia shrugged it off with typical Italian insouciance: her sister was entitled to do anything she wanted — to marry any man she chose to marry.

The Villa Ponti

Few women have ever had their husbands give them a more luxuriously expensive present than Sophia Loren received from Carlo Ponti. It was a Roman villa that Ponti had purchased in the early 1950's.

Later remodeled, added to and decorated, it now contains a four-story guest house built above an old Roman cave, a 135-foot coach-shaped swimming pool, a sauna, a pond with a waterfall and its own little island — and the mansion itself — a 50-room house with fifteen bathrooms, six libraries (some made from the

Two Women

Until 1960, Sophia Loren performed mainly in ordinary movies. Then came the most important film of her life, "Two Women".

Working on this film with Ponti and De Sica, she was forced to recall all the agonies of her childhood . . . and to relive the drama and tragedy of World War II. During many scenes, she was forced to stop the shooting — because of the story's emotional impact on her.

When she was acting the part of a hungry mother, returning to a home that had been bombed, Sophia had merely to recollect her own childhood.

From the very first day of shooting, everyone seemed to realize that "Two Women" was special. There was a reality, an intensity, that occurs only when "acting" ends and true art begins.

The critics agreed. Sophia won awards for

During break in filming of "Black Orchid" (1959) with director Martin Ritt.

Best Actress at Cannes, the New York Film Critics Circle and British Film Academy.

But no foreign language film had ever won an Oscar before. And in 1961 the competition was especially fierce. Audrey Hepburn was the leading contender, as Holly Golightly in "Breakfast at Tiffany's". Geraldine Page was also in the running for "Summer and Smoke" — as was Natalie Wood for "Splendor in the Grass", and Piper Laurie for "The Hustler".

Sophia was so totally convinced that it would be impossible for her to win, that she decided not to travel to Hollywood: besides, it would be a waste of time, for she had begun filming "Boccaccio '70" in Rome.

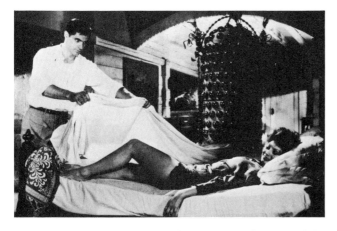

John Gavin tucks in a giddy Sophia in "A Breath of Scandal" (1960).

With Tab Hunter's attention elsewhere, Sophia eases her tired feet in "That Kind of Woman" (1959).

But she did decide to stay up the night of the Academy Awards — and catch the action via wireless.

When the award for Best Actress was announced, Sophia was so overwhelmed that she leaped out of her chair — and ran around kissing everyone in sight. It was an amazing exhibition of youthful exuberance.

The awkward girl from Pozzuoli, whom everybody had once called "toothpick," had earned the highest honor that her peers could bestow!

One Of Us

Few of the world's actresses have the universal appeal that Sophia Loren commands. It is a rare combination of beauty, sensuality, earthiness, sensitivity, warmth and humor.

With equal intensity, she can play mother, wife, mistress and scorned woman. She has played all these roles in real life. She knows them well.

In "Marriage, Italian Style", she revealed her spectacular abilities as a comedienne. Her timing was perfect, her mugging as subtle as Chaplin's, as wildly antic as Groucho Marx's.

In "Two Women", she revealed an intensity of emotion that few people realized till then she possessed. She conveyed the ravages of war, the suffering of humanity, as well as any actor or actress of our time.

In "Arabesque", she created a mood of tension and suspense that an exacting master of suspense, such as Alfred Hitchcock, could applaud.

In "A Perfect Day", she proved that her beauty could survive without make-up. Though the role lacked glamour and romance, her femininity shone through; she evoked a glowing earthiness which few actresses could match.

In "Lady L", she showed her sense of elegance — and contempt for hypocrisy.

In "Boccaccio '70", she revealed a full range of sensuality. Here was a sexiness which left most men limp, while producing in women an equally strong feeling of admiration.

The range of her talents has been truly spectacular.

Whatever role she decides to play —whether it be comedy, drama, social commentary, wild

Fitting costumes for "Heller in Pink Tights" (1960).

Sophia strolls along Manhattan's Seventh Avenue, the fashion district, during a shopping trip, 1959.

sex or suspense — she always brings something very special to the screen: a quality that declares that she is one of us.

From Sex Symbol To Artist

Sophia Loren's range as an actress has grown with each year. She began as a sex goddess, transformed herself into a superb comedienne, then explored the depths of her dramatic talents in some of the most moving portrayals ever seen on the screen. Consider the variety of roles she has played:

140

In "A Special Day," Loren played an overworked, aging housewife in Mussolini's Rome. It was the first role where she wore no make-up at all.

In "Judith," Loren was the Jewish wife of a Nazi war criminal assigned to train Arab terrorists in Damascus. She is denounced to the Nazis by her husband and subsequently seeks revenge. It was the only part Loren ever played that she felt was "totally unbelievable."

"Quo Vadis" was her first film. She played several bit parts, including a slave girl to Deborah Kerr.

Relaxing during the filming of "A Breath of Scandal" (1960), in which Sophia plays a princess.

Onlookers close in on Sophia and Clark Gable during scene from "It Started in Naples" (1960).

In "A Countess from Hong Kong," she played *Natasha*, an aristocratic refugee of the Russian Revolution who stows away in the cabin of a luxury liner on its way to America. A series of romantic complications and adventures ensue. It was her only film with Marlon Brando, and her first chance to work with Charlie Chaplin.

"Yesterday, Today and Tomorrow" is a trilogy in which Loren plays three different women: *Adelina* is arrested for selling contraband, and keeps herself out of jail by keeping herself pregnant! Wealthy and elegant *Anna* is outrageously concerned with her worldly possessions, and *Mara*, the prostitute, falls in love with a seminary student!

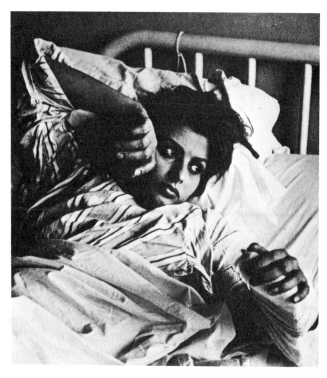

In a pensive mood recovering from a shoulder broken after completion of "El Cid" (1961).

As a sultry laundress in "Madame Sans-Gene" (1961).

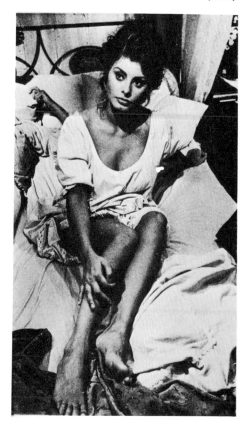

In "Boccaccio '70," she played *Zoe*, a woman who "raffled herself off" every Saturday night at the fair at her brother-in-law's demand. She's the most popular attraction at the fair, but Zoe gives it all up when she falls in love.

Before shooting "Africa Under the Seas," Loren didn't know how to swim. She learned for the part, though, which required that she spend a good deal of her time under water in her role as *Barbara*.

Gina Lollobrigida was originally cast, but Loren eventually assumed the title role in "Aida." Though this was one of Loren's first leading roles, her voice was never heard. Renata Tebaldi dubbed the voice of *Aida*.

In "Two Women," Loren plays *Cesira* who, along with her 13-year-old daughter, makes a perilous journey through Italy during World War II. In an attempt to reach her native village, *Cesira* and child encounter extreme danger and many complications in their lives. Loren's moving portrayal of a mother watching her daughter grow up too quickly, too harshly, won her the Oscar.

In "Attila the Hun", Loren plays *Honoria*, the scheming sister of Emperor Valentinian.

In "Two Nights with Cleopatra," Loren held the title role. Each time she spent the night with an unfortunate member of her guard; he was executed the next morning. But Cesarino's case was different . . .

In "The Miller's Wife," Loren joined together for the first time with Mastroianni and De Sica. This is a light comedy about se-

Sophia "twists" with Mme. Regine, owner of famed Paris discotheque, during filming of "Five Miles to Midnight" (1962).

In "Legend of the Lost," Loren teamed up with John Wayne, who led her through mile after mile of hot, dry desert on a donkey. She played the role of *Dita*, a lusty slave girl. Filmed on location in the Sahara, the film nearly cost Loren her life when a small heater in her hotel room malfunctioned while she was sleeping.

In "Gold of Naples," Loren portrayed a lusty pizza vendor who gets herself in trouble when she loses her wedding ring in a lovers' tryst. Loren caught pneumonia playing the part of *Sofia* and was confined to a sick bed for a month.

In "The Pride and the Passion," Loren spoke her first English words on film. Set in the milieu of the Spanish Army in 1810, this is a story of war and jealous passion in which Loren plays the object of two men's desire in her role as *Juana*.

In "Desire Under the Elms," Loren played *Anna*, the beautiful young bride of an old time New England farmer in this story involving lust, jealousy and fury in the confines of one family.

In "Heller in Pink Tights," Loren plays *Angelu Rossini*, the star of a renegade theater company always running from the law. Her taste for the finer things in life keeps her constantly in debt and devising schemes to pay her bills.

In "A Breath of Scandal," Sophia plays the elegant but sometimes indiscreet princess *Olympia* who is supposed to marry a Russian prince but instead elopes with a Pittsburgh mining engineer. This was a far cry from her earlier roles as a voluptous Italian peasant girl.

duction. The governor tries to take advantage of *Carmela* (Loren), but she is too clever a foil for him.

In "Woman of the River," Loren gave a sensual, wide-ranging dramatic performance that would finally establish her as an important actress. In this film, she played an earthy, sultry, working woman — a role that she would return to many times.

Though "Boy on a Dolphin" was far from a highly acclaimed movie, Loren's performance as *Phaedra*, a Greek peasant girl, was lauded by the critics. In one scene Loren appears on a fishing boat. Suddenly, she gets soaked. The picture of her with her wet clothes clinging to her became one of the most famous posters of all time.

It is hard to imagine a couple more odd than Peter Sellers and Sophia Loren. But that was the starring duo in "The Millionairess" — based on the play by Bernard Shaw. Loren is heiress to an industrial empire and the man she chooses to marry is a poor Indian doctor. Before they marry, they each put the other to a test whose results cause a lot of confusion.

In "Madame," Sophia had the part of *Catherine*, a boisterous, beautiful washerwoman who rises to become the Duchess of Danzig during the Napoleonic Wars. Portraying that astonishing transformation was a challenge even to her maturing skills as an actress. She handled it admirably.

"The Journey," based on a story by Luigi Pirandello, teamed Richard Burton with Sophia Loren. This was the 30th picture directed by Vittorio De Sica, but even before the filming had begun, two complications set in. Firstly, just prior to the start of the picture, De Sica collapsed with a serious lung illness. Ponti, his lifelong friend, quickly took action. He contacted a surgeon and team of doctors in Switzerland, chartered a plane in Rome and flew De Sica to the doctors. When he was well enough to return to work, Ponti arranged for medical aid to be available on the set.

The second interruption in the filming was that the volatile Mr. and Mrs. Burton broke up in a fury and a frenzy, were apart and separately despondent, (during which time Richard was the house guest of the Ponti's), and re-united.

In the film, Sophia played a peasant Sicilian widow who has a serious heart ailment. Her brother-in-law (Burton) takes her to various specialists whose only advice is to enjoy life to the fullest. She experiences life and love as she has never known it, concluding on the day Archduke Francis Ferdinand is assassinated. They know the world will never again be as innocent

Supporting Tony Perkins on the set of "Five Miles to Midnight" (1962).

Deglamorized in de Sica's "Yesterday, Today and Tomorrow" (1963).

In "Marriage, Italian Style," her partnership with Marcello Mastroianni truly blossomed. Marcello played a wealthy playboy; Sophia was his beautiful mistress. The movie follows their relationship over a period of years until she finally traps him into marriage.

In "The Priest's Wife," Sophia tries to woo Mastroianni away from the church. It brought howls from the audience and cries of anguish from the pulpit.

In "The White Sister," she was on the other side, becoming *Sister Germana*, the guiding force of a Libyan missionary hospital. Here, Loren, one of the world's most alluring women, was totally convincing as a nun.

"Our Times" is a potpourri of vignettes ranging from the poignant to the comic. Sophia plays an alluring model for a very admiring photographer.

An unsuspecting cab driver is duped time and again by Loren's *Lina* in "Too Bad She's Bad". A routine cab ride reveals that *Lina*

and her family are trying to steal the taxi! After putting up with much conniving and trickery on the part of *Lina* and clan, the driver, (Marcello Mastroianni) hauls them to the police. A lot of fast talk on *Lina's* part gets her out of trouble with the police and married to the driver!

Loren played *Argriese*, an innocently alluring girl who is constantly surrounded by suitors in "The Sign of Venus." Her cousin Cesira, a plainer girl, is more ambitious in her pursuit of a man, but less successful. This was a light role for Loren in which she shared the limelight with Franca Valeri.

Striking an imperial pose with Alec Guinness in "The Fall of the Roman Empire" (1964).

In a harem costume, "Marriage — Italian Style" (1964).

In "Scandal in Sorrento," Loren plays *Donna Sofia*, the local fish vendor who gets what she wants (including a place to live and a man to marry) by using her all-conquering charm.

"Lucky To Be a Woman" is a romantic story in which Loren plays *Antoinette*, a girl who reaches stardom through the efforts of a photographer, who is in love with her. He waits patiently in the wings while she explores her newfound fame. But Antoinette realizes in the end that her love for him is more important than a flashy career.

Loren stars as *Rose Bianco* in "Black Orchid". *Rose* is a widow living in New York and just making ends meet. She is on the threshold of remarrying when her future husband's (Anthony Quinn) daughter steps in and creates problems for them.

Marcello Mastroianni clowns with Sophia in "Marriage — Italian Style" (1964).

After filming "Judith" (1965) in Israel, Sophia tours Jerusalem.

Posing as a widowed countess in "Lady L . . ." (1965).

Trying on shoes for "Arabesque" (1966).

In "That Kind of Woman," Loren plays a high class "mistress" named *Kay* who is employed by a millionaire to entertain generals and the like. When a lowly G.I. falls in love with her and pursues her, she has to decide between the life of luxury she's been leading and the young soldier's affections. Love wins after all.

In "It Started in Naples," Loren plays a hot nightclub dancer *Lucia* who's taking care of her orphaned nephew Nando. When Mike (Clark Gable) appears on the scene to settle his late brother's affairs, he discovers that Nando is actually his brother's child. Appalled at the "delinquent" manner in which *Lucia* is bringing up the child, he insists on taking Nando back to America. In the ensuing custody battle, Mike and Lucia fall in love.

"Houseboat" teamed Cary Grant and Sophia who, by a strange turn of affairs, end up setting up housekeeping aboard a rundown houseboat with a trio of kids. This was considered one of Sophia's more "natural" American films.

"Arabesque" brought Gregory Peck and Sophia together in an intriguing and complicated story concerning an American professor at Oxford, an oil magnate, a Middle Eastern premier and an exotic woman. Assassination, death, or the threat of death, by a pair of scissors and a wrecking crane, and decoding of an ancient hieroglyphic code are all worked into the plot.

It is a measure of her abilities that Sophia's sexiness can be submerged — when she must play a role that's totally intellectual. She can play old as well as young, saints as well as sinners, glamorous showgirls as well as dowdy housewives. Perhaps the perfect test of any actress is this: how can she survive aging? Sophia Loren has already passed this test. She is now in her mid-40's, and she continues to play roles of astonishing power, sensitivity, and (when needed) sexiness.

Mama Sophia

In the film, "Yesterday, Today and Tomorrow", Sophia portrayed a pregnant woman. It was a role she had yearned for in real life, and she acted the part with uncanny feeling.

Affectionately hugging Carlo during filming of "The Condemned of Altona" (1962).

147

Soon after her marriage to Carlo Ponti, she realized that her life would never be complete until she had children — his children. (Carlo had children from his first marriage.)

The Pontis first attempts to have children were possibly the most highly publicized miscarriages in history. Millions of people read the papers when Sophia was rushed to the hospital.

The first press releases said she had a toothache; then they told the true story: Sophia had lost her baby.

Her second miscarriage — after four months of pregnancy — evoked a torrent of sympathy from her fans all over the world.

Letters flooded into the Villa Ponti, suggesting all sorts of aids: eat nothing but bananas . . .

A meditative moment on the set of "Countess from Hong Kong" (1966).

take Vitamin E . . . always try to get pregnant on the night of a full moon . . . drink orange juice five times a day . . . check your hormones.

This last piece of advice turned out to be the key. A good friend of Sophia's — who had also lost two babies — suggested a famous Swiss specialist, Dr. Hubert de Watteville. Dr. de Watteville examined Sophia, and advised her that, happily, there was no physical reason that she could not have children. However, once she became pregnant, she would require total rest — total peace.

A few months later, the pregnancy occurred — and Dr. de Watteville decided that Sophia should be in a hotel near him. Thus began one of the great scoop-hunting expeditions in the history of Italian journalism.

As soon as she left, reporters noticed Sophia's absence. They beseiged her family with questions: "Where is she?" . . . "Is she planning a divorce from Ponti?"

Sworn to secrecy, her mother and sister refused to reveal her whereabouts: Sophia was in total seclusion in the Swiss hotel recommended by Dr. de Watteville, lying in bed for all but four hours every day.

Few famous people know what the word "privacy" really means. Sophia Loren was not to be one of them.

For eight months, Sophia remained in her room, simply resting and waiting. No reporters, no stars, no friends visited her. Even her mother and sister waited until just before the baby came before they arrived.

Her only attendants were her secretary, her doctor (who had prescribed this nearly total lying in), and, of course, Carlo Ponti.

Of this unusual experience, Sophia later said, "I think about that period I spent in Geneva with some melancholy, no make it nostalgia. It was more than nice; it was one of the most beautiful times of my life, a beautiful experience. Now, when I think that I spent eight months in a room without ever going out just because I was pregnant, I cannot believe it."

Unfortunately, a maid discovering Sophia's secret sold the information to a local newspaper. The subsequent madness could easily have passed as a scenario for a Marx Brothers' movie.

Playing a peasant girl in "Happily Ever After" (1967).

On Saturday, December 28, 1968, Carlo Ponti, Jr., was born. Actually, his full name was Hubert Leoni Carlo Ponti, Jr. — in honor of the doctor who helped Sophia secure the most important role of her life, the role of mother.

"This boy has a great sense of humor," was Carlo's first comment when he saw his son. Sophia's sister Maria was a bit more effusive. "I hadn't seen Sophia for eight months. That afternoon, when I saw her with the baby, I cried all the more, and so did Sophia."

Carlo Jr. became the most important thing in Sophia's life. For a while, he also became something of an obsession.

Every sound he made was studied. "Is he sick?" "Is he choking?" Every time the phone rang, Sophia was afraid it might be a kidnapper or an extortionist.

Sophia's anxiety was something all her close friends and associates endured. Her personal photographer recalls: "I was there one day when

Reporters swarmed to Switzerland and tried to gain entry into Sophia's hotel room. Reporters went so far as to try to get jobs as hotel busboys. Or local policemen. Or waitresses. Anything to get an exclusive interview.

Sophia remained in seclusion through it all. Her pregnancy was proceeding on schedule. At one point, she experienced severe pains — and she was afraid that she was going to lose the baby. But Dr. de Watteville quickly administered an injection of estrogen. The pains went away; the baby was safe.

A few months into her pregnancy, Dr. de Watteville brought a high-powered amplifier into her room, along with a stethoscope. He placed the stethoscope against Sophia's stomach. He listened for a few minutes, twisted a few dials and then Sophia heard — faintly but distinctly — the rhythmic sound of her baby's heartbeat. Tears welled up in her eyes as the sound continued.

Sophia and her mother at the premiere of "Happily Ever After" (1967).

As Sister Germana in "The White Sister" (1971).

Carlo's crying grew a little faint. Sophia was afraid he was losing his voice. A Swiss nurse, Ruth Bapst, explained that she'd given orange juice to the baby, that the acidity of Vitamin C makes the voice go down. I assured Sophia, 'Yes, it's happened with mine, particularly when the juice is cold. It lasts about two hours.' Sophia looked at me as if I'd saved her life."

One of Sophia's severest frights occured a few months after Carlo, Jr. was born. While winding up a crib toy, Sophia broke part of it — and the broken part landed on little Carlo.

"Naturally, I snatched him up right away. And he cried so much that for awhile he couldn't breathe," Sophia later said of the incident. "It hadn't hurt him much or done him any harm, but I'm sure he reacted because he could feel my own terror."

Sophia's love for her little boy was so strong that it frequently outweighed other obligations. One evening shortly after Carlo was born, she and Carlo Sr. went to a play — and almost left before it was over.

"I began to wonder what I was doing in a theatre when I had a child at home who was all I was thinking about . . . I wanted to leave after the first act, but I had to stay. Everyone knew I was there, and, if I didn't come back, it would have become 'The Play She Walked Out On,'" Sophia later said.

Eventually, as Sophia grew accustomed to

motherhood, she took in stride things that alarmed others.

At 3 a.m. one day, a maid woke Sophia with the news that the baby was screaming. A few seconds later, a smiling Sophia said, "Why, he was just practicing his screams. But I think I'll go look at him — and maybe I'll tape-record him."

She spoke of her little son's screaming in greater detail in 1969. "He'd just discovered the sound of his own voice, and he screamed because he wanted to listen to all the noises he could make. He was so happy with them that you knew nothing was the matter. He was busy discovering his own reactions and the day just wasn't long enough."

On January 1, 1973, four years after Carlo Jr. was born, the Pontis had their second child, Eduardo. Life was now complete for Sophia.

Like the devoted mother that she is, Sophia Loren is always concerned that she's not spending enough time with her sons.

En route from Paris, where she's starring in "The Verdict" (1974) to Ankara for Turkish opening of "The Voyage" (1973).

The Pontis.

One day, to see how he would react, she told young Carlo Jr., "I don't want to be an actress anymore."

"You're kidding," young Carlo responded, "It's the most beautiful profession in the world. You should never quit."

That settled the matter.

Sophia Loren has proven that she can play three roles: mother, wife, and actress. And play them all superbly!

After 20 Years

The marriage between Sophia Loren and Carlo Ponti has been one of the most successful in filmdom. What keeps them so totally committed to each other?

The answer lies largely in the temperament of Sophia Loren. When she undertakes a project, she does it with a total dedication that few people understand.

She entered into marriage with the same sense of total dedication.

Sophia is fully aware how much a father her husband is. She understands that her marriage to Carlo is, in many ways, a marriage to the father she never had. She has expressed this many times.

Sophia also respects and accepts Carlo as her mentor. If he decides that she must go from comedienne to serious actress, she never questions his judgement. If he suggests that she read such classics as *Don Quixote* and *The Red and the Black,* she follows his suggestions.

Raised without a father, Sophia observed her mother's yearning for the love and companionship that only a man can bring. When Carlo gave up his wife and children to marry Sophia, she thoroughly comprehended the sacrifice he had made, the total dedication he must have for her to have made it.

Sophia, expressing her strong feelings about Carlo, has remarked: "He is father, husband, lover, big brother, confidant — and, above all, my best friend. I would have to be mad to risk losing him to seek a few moments of pleasure with another man. And I know Carlo is true to me, as I am to him. He found me and helped me to where I am today. He has always been right for me, then and now."

Sophia at 1979 press party for release of her autobiography "Living and Loving."

THE FILMS OF SOPHIA LOREN

4

The Films of Sophia Loren

QUO VADIS 1950 (MGM). The cast included Robert Taylor, Peter Ustinov, Deborah Kerr and Leo Genn. Director was Mervyn LeRoy.

HEARTS UPON THE SEA 1950 (Cine-Albatros). The cast included Doris Dowling, Jacques Sernas, and Milly Vitale. Director was Giorgio Bianchi.

THE VOTE 1950 (ARA). The cast included Georgio de Lullo and Doris Duranti. Director was Mario Bonnard.

BLUEBEARD'S SIX WIVES 1950 (Golden). The cast included Toto, Luigi Parese and Isa Barzizza. Director was Carlo Ludovico.

10 SONO IL CAPATZ 1950 (Jolly). The cast included Silvana Pampanini and Marilyn Buferd. Director was Giorgio Simonelli.

MILANA THE MILLIONAIRESS 1951 (Mambretti). The cast included Toni Scotti and Isa Barzizza. Director was Fictorrio Metz.

ANNA 1951 (Archway). The cast included Silvana Mangano, Raf Vallone and Vittorio Gassman. Director was Alberto Lattuada.

THE MAGICIAN IN SPITE OF HIMSELF 1951 (Amati-Mambretti). The cast included Toni Scotti, Dorian Gray, and Mirella Umberti. Director was Vittorio Metz.

THE DREAM OF ZORRO 1951 (ICS). The cast included Vittorio Gassman, Walter Chiari and Michele Philippe. Director was Mario Soldati.

THE PIANO TUNER HAS ARRIVED 1951 (Itala/Titanus). The cast included Alberto Sordi, Nino Tarranti and Tamara Lees. Director was Duilio Coletti.

IT'S HIM, YES! YES! 1951 (Amati). The cast included Walter Chiari, Silvana Pampanini and Fanfulla. Director was Vittorio Metz.

THE FAVORITE 1952 (MAS). The cast included Gino Sinimberghi, Franca Tamantini and Paolo Silveri. Director was Cesare Barlacchi.

Selling pizza in "Gold of Naples" (1954).

154

As Cleopatra in "Two Nights With Cleopatra" (1953).

AFRICA UNDER THE SEAS 1952 (Gala). The cast included Steve Barclay and Umberto Malnati. Director was Giovanni Roccardi.

THE WHITE SLAVE TRADE 1952 (Excelsa/Ponti-De Laurentiis). The cast included Vittorio Gassman, Silvana Pampanini, Bruno Rossini and Ettore Manni. Director was Luigi Comencini.

AIDA 1953 (Eagle). The cast included Giulio Neri and Renata Tebaldi. Director was Clemente Fracassi.

GOOD PEOPLE'S SUNDAY 1953 (Trionfalcine). The cast included Maria Fiore, Carlo Romano and Renato Salvatori. Director was Anton Majano.

THE COUNTRY OF BELLS 1953 (Valentina). The cast included Carlo Dapporto and Alda Mangini. Director was Jean Boyer.

A DAY IN COURT 1953 (Excelsa/Documents). The cast included Silvana Pampanini, Alberto Sordi, Walter Chiari and Leopoldo Trieste. Director was Steno.

PILGRIM OF LOVE 1953 (Pisorno). The cast included Alda Mangini, Enrico Viarisio and Charles Rutherford. Director was Andrea Forzano.

NEAPOLITAN CAROUSEL 1953 (Archway). The cast included Vera Nandi, Paolo Stoppa and Leonide Massine. Director was Ettore Giannini.

WE'LL MEET IN THE GALLERY 1953 (Athene-Enic). The cast included Alberto Sordi, Carlo Dapporto and Nilla Pizzi. Director was Mauro Bolognini.

ANATOMY OF LOVE 1953. The cast included Vittorio De Sica and Marcello Mastroianni. Director was Alessandro Blasetti.

TWO NIGHTS WITH CLEOPATRA 1953 (Excelsa-Rosa). The cast included Alberto Sordi, Ettore Manni and Paul Muller. Director was Mario Mattoli.

ATILLA THE HUN 1953 (Archway). The cast included Anthony Quinn, Irene Papas, Henri Vidal and Ettore Manni. Director was Pietro Francisci.

GOLD OF NAPLES 1954 (Gala). The cast included Giacomo Furia, Alberto Farnes and Paolo Stoppa. Director was Vittorio De Sica.

WOMAN OF THE RIVER 1954 (Columbia). The cast included Rik Battaglia, Gerard Oury and Lise Bourdin. Director was Mario Soldati.

Drenched and still gorgeous in "Boy on a Dolphin" (1957).

POVERTY AND NOBILITY 1954 (Excelsa). The cast included Toto, Franca Faldini and Enzo Turco. Director was Mario Mattoli.

TOO BAD SHE'S BAD 1954 (Gala). The cast included Vittorio De Sica, Marcello Mastroianni, and Umberto Malmatti. Director was Alessandro Blasetti.

THE SIGN OF VENUS 1955 (Gala). The cast included Vittorio De Sica, Raf Vallone and Alberto Sordi. Director was Dino Risi.

THE MILLER'S WIFE 1955 (Gala). The cast included Vittorio De Sica, Marcello Mastroianni, Paolo Stoppa and Yvonne Sanson. Director was Mario Camerini.

SCANDAL IN SORRENTO 1955 (Gala). The cast included Vittorio De Sica, Lea Padovani, Antonio Cifariello and Tina Pica. Director was Dino Risi.

LUCKY TO BE A WOMAN 1955 (Intercontinental). The cast included Charles Boyer, Marcello Mastroianni, Nino Besozzi and Titina Di Filippo. Director was Alessandro Blasetti.

THE PRIDE AND THE PASSION 1957 (United Artists). The cast included Cary Grant, Frank Sinatra, Theodore Bikel and Jose Nicto. Director was Stanley Kramer.

BOY ON A DOLPHIN 1957 (20th Century-Fox). The cast included Alan Ladd, Clifton Webb, Alexis Minotis and Jorge Mistral. Director was Jean Negulesco.

LEGEND OF THE LOST 1957 (United Artists). The cast included John Wayne, Rossano Brazzi and Kurt Kaznar. Director was Henry Hathaway.

DESIRE UNDER THE ELMS 1958 (Paramount). The cast included Anthony Perkins, Burl Ives, Frank Overton, Pernell Roberts and Anne Seymour. Director was Delbert Mann.

HOUSEBOAT 1958 (Paramount/Scribe). The cast included Cary Grant, Martha Hyer, Harry Guardino, Paul Peterson and Werner Klemperer. Director was Melville Shavelson.

THE KEY 1958 (Columbia Pictures). The cast included William Holden, Oscar Homolka, Trevor Howard, Kieron Moore and Beatrix Lehman. Director was Carol Reed.

THE BLACK ORCHID 1959 (Paramount). The cast included Anthony Quinn, Ina Balin and Jimmy Baird. Director was Martin Ritt.

THAT KIND OF WOMAN 1959 (Paramount). The cast included Tab Hunter, Jack Warden, George Sanders, Barbara Nichols and Keenan Wynn. Director was Sidney Lumet.

HELLER IN PINK TIGHTS 1960 (Paramount). The cast included Anthony Quinn, Steve Forrest, Eileen Heckart, Margaret O'Brien and Edmund Lowe. Director was George Cukor.

IT STARTED IN NAPLES 1960 (Paramount). The cast included Clark Gable, Vittorio De Sica, Marietto and Paolo Carlini. Director was Melville Shavelson.

A BREATH OF SCANDAL 1960 (Paramount). The cast included John Gavin, Angela Lansbury, Isabel Jeans and Maurice Chevalier. Director was Michael Curtiz.

With Eleanor Brown, who plays her daughter, in "Two Women" (1960).

Sophia uses judo to make Dennis Price behave in "The Millionairess" (1960).

THE MILLIONAIRESS 1960 (20th Century-Fox). The cast included Peter Sellers, Alastair Sim, Vittorio De Sica, Dennis Price and Gary Raymond. Director was Anthony Asquith.

TWO WOMEN 1961 (Gala). The cast included Jean-Paul Belmondo, Eleanor Brown and Raf Vallone. Director was Vittorio De Sica.

EL CID 1961 (Rank). The cast included Charlton Heston, Herbert Lom, John Fraser and Raf Vallone. Director was Anthony Mann.

BOCCACCIO '70 1961 (Embassy Pictures via 20th Century-Fox). The cast included Luigi Giuliani and Alfio Vita. Director was Vittorio De Sica.

MADAME SANS-GENE 1961 (Embassy Pictures via 20th Century-Fox). The cast included Robert Hossein, Julien Bertheau, Marina Berti and Carlo Giuffere. Director was Christian Jacque.

FIVE MILES TO MIDNIGHT 1962 (United Artists). The cast included Jean-Pierre Aumont, Anthony Perkins, Gig Young, Yolande Turner and Mathilde Casdesus. Director was Anatole Litvak.

THE CONDEMNED OF ALTONA 1962 (20th Century-Fox). The cast included Fredric March, Maximilian Schell and Robert Wagner. Director was Vittorio De Sica.

YESTERDAY, TODAY AND TOMORROW 1963 (Embassy Pictures via Paramount). The cast included Marcello Mastroianni, Aldo Giuffre and Agostino Salvietti. Director was Vittorio De Sica.

THE FALL OF THE ROMAN EMPIRE 1964 (Rank). The cast included Alec Guinness, James Mason, Omar Sharif, Christopher Plummer, Stephen Boyd and Anthony Quayle. Director was Anthony Mann.

MARRIAGE, ITALIAN STYLE 1964 (Embassy Pictures via Paramount). The cast included Marcello Mastroianni, Aldo Puglisi and Tecla Scarano. Director was Vittorio De Sica.

JUDITH 1965 (Paramount). The cast included Peter Finch, Jack Hawkins and Hans Verner. Director was Daniel Mann.

OPERATION CROSSBOW 1965 (MGM/Carlo Ponti). The cast included Trevor Howard, George Peppard, Lilli Palmer, Tom Courtenay, John Mills and Paul Henreid. Director was Michael Anderson.

LADY L 1965 (MGM). The cast included Paul Newman, David Niven, Claude Dauphin, Philippe Noiret and Michel Piceli. Director was Peter Ustinov.

ARABESQUE 1966 (Rank/Universal). The cast included Gregory Peck, Alan Badel and Kieron Moore. Director was Stanley Donen.

A COUNTESS FROM HONG KONG 1966 (Rank/Universal). The cast included Marlon Brando, Sydney Chaplin, Tippi Hedren and Michael Medwin. Director was Charles Chaplin.

HAPPILY EVER AFTER 1967. The cast included Omar Sharif. Director was Francesco Rosi.

GHOSTS, ITALIAN STYLE 1967 (MGM). The cast included Vittorio Gassman, Mario Adorf and Margaret Lee. Director was Renato Castellani.

SUNFLOWER 1969 (Avco Embassy). The cast included Marcello Mastroianni, Ludmila Savelyeva and Anna Carena. Director was Vittorio De Sica.

THE PRIEST'S WIFE 1970 (Warner Brothers). The cast included Marcello Mastroianni and Venantino Venantini. Director was Dino Risi.

An affectionate moment with Marcello Mastroianni in "Sunflower" (1969).

LADY LIBERTY 1971 (Warner Brothers). The cast included William Devane, Luigi Proietti and Beeson Carroll. Director was Mario Monicelli.

WHITE SISTER 1971 (Columbia-Warner). The cast included Adriano Celentano, Fernando Rey and Luis Marin. Director was Alberto Lattuada.

MAN OF LA MANCHA 1972 (United Artists). The cast included Peter O'Toole, Ian Richardson and James Coco. Director was Arthur Hiller.

THE VOYAGE 1973 (United Artists). The cast included Richard Burton, Ian Bannen and Paolo Lena. Director was Vittorio De Sica.

VERDICT 1974 (Les Films Concordia/Champion). The cast included Jean Gabin, Henri Garcia and Julien Bertheau. Director was Andre Cayatte.

Well-disguised as a desperate woman, Sophia strides through a poor section of Rome in "Yesterday, Today and Tomorrow" (1963).

The waitress behind the bar? Sophia, in "Angela" (1976).

BRIEF ENCOUNTER 1974. The cast included Richard Burton.
Director was Alan Bridges.

GUN MOLL 1974. The cast included Marcello Mastroianni.
Director was Giorgio Capitani.

A SPECIAL DAY 1975. The cast included Marcello Mastroianni.
Director was Ettore Scola.

CASSANDRA CROSSING 1976. The cast included Richard Harris,
Ava Gardner and Burt Lancaster. Director was George Pan
Cosmatos.

ANGELA 1976. The cast included John Huston, John Vernon and
Steve Railsback. Director was Boris Sagal.

BRASS TARGET 1978. The cast included George Kennedy, Robert
Vaughn, Max Von Sydow and John Cassavettes. Director was John
Hough.

FIRE POWER 1979. The cast included James Coburn and O.J.
Simpson. Director was Michael Winner.

A BLOOD FEUD 1979. The cast included Marcello Mastroianni
and Giancarlo Giannini. Director was Lina Wertmuller.

Victor Mature with Sophia in "Fire Power" (1979), shot on
Manhattan's East Side.